Freedom From My Past
The Power of Forgiveness

Jeanette Ekberg

Urban Press
PUBLISHING YOUR DREAMS

Freedom From My Past
by Jeanette Ekberg
Copyright ©2024 Jeanette Ekberg

ISBN 978-1-63360-290-8

Unless otherwise noted, scripture quotations are taken from the Easy-to-Read Version Bible. Copyright © 2006 by Bible League international.

Scripture quotations marked TLB are taken from The Living Bible copyright © 1971 by Tyndale House Foundation. Used by permission of Tyndale House Publishers Inc., Carol Stream, Illinois 60188. All rights reserved.

Scripture quotations marked NKJV are taken from the New King James Version®. Copyright © 1982 by Thomas Nelson. Used by permission. All rights reserved.

For Worldwide Distribution
Printed in the U.S.A.

Urban Press
P.O. Box 8881
Pittsburgh, PA 15221-0881
412.646.2780
www.urbanpress.us

Contents

Dedication

This book is dedicated with great love and appreciation to my husband and best friend, Dan Ekberg. His support, encouragement, and love have been invaluable and have encouraged me and made me a better person. I could not have written this book without him.

Acknowledgements

So many people were helpful to me in the writing process.

- My former pastor, talented writer, publisher, and friend, John Stanko, and President of PurposeQuest International from Pennsylvania, who walked me through every step of the way.

- The pastors, teachers and staff at our beloved Grace Family Church in Land O' Lakes, Florida who encouraged me—especially the teacher of the *Freedom* class, Debbie Pitcock, who prayed with me in the forgiveness process—to believe in myself enough to write this book.

- Susie Walther, founder of *The Well*, a women's training ministry in Land O' Lakes, Florida. She also prayed with me and helped me to understand that by writing this book, I should feel that there is no guilt or condemnation to keep me from it.

- I should also thank my close friend, Marty Stewart, who sat with me for hours, letting me share all my deepest secrets with her and she never judged me and Dara Snowden who stayed in contact with me all these years and provided us with valuable medical information for the treatment of Dan's health issues.

- Thank you also to my friend of over 30 years who is also a writer, Diana Scimone. She jump started me and led me on the path to write this book. I don't think I would have attempted it without her support and encouragement.

INTRODUCTION

I'm not a writer. I am a wife, a mother, a sister, and a friend. I'm sharing my testimony so that perhaps it can help just one person who is going through, or has been through, anything like I have. I know I'm not the only one to have gone through trials and pain. But I was never comfortable until now sharing my story because I have always been ashamed of the things I have done and/or been through.

When I was weak and hopeless, God held on to me as His child. Faith is what got me to this point, because I no longer believed the lies that Satan had led me to believe. I know now that I'm a child of God, and He has always been my one true, loving Father.

Even when I turned my back on Him, He never left me. He loved me enough to bring me through despite my sin. I didn't understand why I went through what I did at the time, but I know now that I did not go through any of it alone. I may be repetitious, but God was always there with me. As a child, I always knew there was a God, I just didn't think He knew me.

With Jesus, I have learned that there is no shame or condemnation. His blood has washed us clean, and we are sinless in His eyes. I have been redeemed. I am not who I used to be. God never promised us that there would not be storms, but He promised that He would always be there to help us through. The trials and issues I have endured proved to me that I am alive because of the love, presence, and power of God and my faith in Him.

In this book, I will tell various stories about my life. I will talk about the physical and mental abuse I endured. I was continually being told I would never be anything; that I was worthless. I was so ashamed. But that is who I was, not who I am. I am now a new being, a new woman in Christ. And I want to spread the good news with you in case you haven't learned it, or you need to be reminded. You are His—isn't that good news?

This book will walk through my childhood. I will not rehash the past but reveal how Christ has set me free. I want you to know what I have been set free from. So, let's get started with my journey.

Jeanette Ekberg
Land O' Lakes, Florida
December 2024

Chapter 1

THE BEGINNING

I was born in Rochester, New York. I don't remember much about living with my biological father because he left us when we were young. My mom and he divorced. This is when my story began.

Biologically speaking, I have two older sisters. We are about a year apart. I have a younger brother. He is two years younger than I. My two sisters left home when they got older, and they were able to get out on their own. Because I was the younger one, I stayed to protect the others from being treated as badly as we had been.

My mother was mean. I think her mother, my grandmother, was that way also. She was from Managua, Nicaragua, and she was a very hateful and mean-spirited woman. After years of abuse, I felt as if I wasn't worth anything. I was a piece of trash because that's what I had been repeatedly told.

My dad was a cheater. Once, my mother told him that if he could tell her that he wouldn't cheat anymore, they could make things work. He said, "I can't promise you that." So they divorced.

Mom worked constantly which I give her credit for. She was a hard worker, but we had to do everything around the house. Often we got stuck with babysitters. Most often, they would have their boyfriends over. We would spy on them and they would chase us and beat us with fly swatters.

Then Mom came home one day with a big Italian, scary-looking guy. She said, "This is going to be your new dad." After my mom's big announcement, we ran to our bedrooms crying because we were scared to death and quite upset. We were five, maybe six or seven years old. My brother was even younger than that.

That's how old we were when he started playing the games with us. For a while he took care of himself (if you know what I mean). But, then he had us taking care of him. We didn't realize what was happening. We were running around in my mother's half-slips like they were gowns, and we had on her high heels. We were having a ball, and he loved watching us do that. When we got a little bit older, my oldest sister realized something was not right with what he was doing. She went to our mother and told her what he had been doing. She either didn't believe her or she blamed us. I don't know exactly what she was thinking, but it was a typical response from her.

My biological dad remarried another woman, and she got pregnant. He claims he didn't know she was pregnant when he left her. Eventually, he divorced her and married a third wife. We found out about the child that his second wife had when that child was 38 years old. My dad never told us. We went all those years not knowing him and he never knew he had half-brothers and sisters.

My dad would come pick us up occasionally to take us for the day, but we didn't see much of him. My mom always made it hard on him. She would send my grandmother with him to make sure he was behaving. I don't know why. He wasn't abusive. The real problem was Mom's new husband, not our father. I'm not sure why she didn't feel a need to protect us from him.

Dad's third wife already had a son and a daughter when they married. Those kids were his priority. His main focus became all about her and the two kids while we took a back seat. We would fight with those two when we were together. They'd call him "Dad," and we would let them know that he was our dad. It was a very uncomfortable relationship.

I hated school where I got teased all the time. My two front teeth were crossed, and I was tall, skinny, and flat-chested. I wore my bangs down to hide my face. I was not popular and never had a boyfriend. I hung out with the ugly girls. It was terrible.

I would report that I was sick every Monday and Friday, so I only had to go to school for three days. I'd stick my finger down my throat and make myself throw up so I didn't have to go to school. Eventually, I got to where I didn't even have to stick my finger down my throat. I could just make myself throw up without any help.

I hated school so much and I almost didn't graduate. My history teacher pitied me because he had my other two sisters ahead of me and he liked them. They were decent students. I had to get a "D" in my class to graduate. I had "Fs" all the way, but he gave me a "D" so I could graduate.

Even as I write this, it brings up such bad memories, but they don't overwhelm me. As I wrote in the Introduction, I am free—free from my past and the things that bound me for many years. However, there is more of my story that needs to be told and it's not pretty, just like this chapter wasn't. Let me continue with my saga in the next chapter.

To lighten the story a bit, let me share some things I now know about my past and about myself that the Lord has shown me over the last few years. These truths helped me, and I know they will help you if you are going through anything remotely close to what I did.

Chapter 2

THE STRUGGLE

I was young, I don't remember all the details, but I do remember the general story. Mom ended up moving us out to her mother's and dad's house in the country in Canandaigua, New York. It is a town on Canandaigua Lake. It was a small house. We were crowded, but it was a picturesque family home.

Mom and the four of us kids lived with my grandmother, my grandfather, their son (my mother's brother). It didn't take long to realize that the arrangement was not working out. My grandmother was mean and nasty, as stated earlier, and she hated having us living there with them. Eventually, my mother moved us all back in with my stepfather. She said we had moved for financial reasons, but no reason could justify the misery of that move.

My stepdad swore the inappropriate behavior would stop. He said he wouldn't bother us anymore. But in no time at all, it started up again. He scared the pants off us—literally. We were scared to death of him. He would threaten us with punishment if we didn't cooperate. He never had sexual intercourse with us, thank goodness, but he did everything else he could think of. My two sisters eventually moved out. However, my mom had five more kids with him, and I felt obligated to try and protect them.

More contention followed when my sisters moved out. There was an incident in which my mother tried to drown my little sister. And, in another incident, she beat my brother until he fell to the floor, then she kicked him. If we left our books on the dining room table or left our bicycles out, she would come, drag us out of bed in the middle of the night and pound on us. I remember that we were all well behaved in our early years. As we got older, however, we were not exactly angels! Once we were caught leaning out our bedroom window smoking. The neighbor across the street saw us and let Mom know. That was a bad idea on our part.

I was a Catholic with a lot of guilt and shame. I had no self-esteem whatsoever. I felt like a piece of garbage. My mom would make us go to religious instruction after school, and we'd have to go to confession on Saturday and communion on Sunday. My mom never went to church because she said she was excommunicated from Catholicism for being divorced.

I brought holy water home from church and put a little bowl outside my bedroom door. I told my sister she had to anoint herself before she could come inside my room. She refused and made fun of me for making that declaration. I was hoping the holy water would protect me and us. It didn't.

The desperation to be free and cleansed was so great that there was a time in my life when I wanted to be a nun because I thought maybe God could help me. I only knew God from what I had read. I knew it in my head, not in my heart where the words count and take root. I was never asked to accept Him as my Lord and Savior until later in my life.

I knew God created us, and I wondered why He would create us to let us go through so many trials and tribulations. Anyway, Mom wouldn't go to church. She had no spiritual compass. She dropped us off and we'd have to walk home, about two miles, because she never came back to pick us up.

I was so ashamed of what my stepdad was doing to me. We were all made to feel guilty as if everything was our fault. I couldn't tell anyone outside of the house about what was going on, mostly because of the shame, but mainly because of his threats. We believed he would follow through on his promises of violence.

The irony is that he never touched his own kids. I had planned to stay to protect my younger brother, but he bounced back and forth between families, so he wasn't always with us. He would stay with whoever treated him better. He wasn't included in the chaos. He didn't know about anything. I stayed longer to protect the Reales, the little kids or Mom's "second litter" as I labeled them. (Our stepfather's children were the Reales.) It wasn't our stepdad that I had to protect them from, it was from my mother. She kicked me out because I interfered with her form of discipline, which was really punishment bordering on torture.

My mother would say she couldn't wait until it was just the Reales left in the house. She couldn't wait to get rid of everything from marriage number one. My biological dad was paying child support, not a lot, but he paid for the four of us until we turned 18. It had become apparent that I was coming between my mother and the other kids, and she didn't like that. Before she evicted me, she said, "You're undermining my authority." That was one of her famous sayings.

As soon as we all turned 18, my mom said, "Get out." I had been making payments on a car of Mom's I used to drive to school because we had moved out of our district, and I wanted to graduate there. When my mom told me to leave, she said, "Don't think you're taking the car." I simply replied, "Okay." What was the point of arguing? It made me sad to think that all the money I paid went down the drain. After that, I had to call my sister for a ride. She came to get me and took me to my dad's house to live with him and my stepmom. They were very good to me. No problems existed between me and my stepmom; she treated me well.

There was a weird occasion at their house that I remember. My stepbrother was a real weirdo. He liked to get into our drawers and wear our underwear. He would soil them, and then put them back in the dresser drawer, although he denied it. His mother wouldn't hear of it, believing he would never do anything like that. Eventually, my step-sister and I moved out and got a place together. That didn't last long because I didn't care for her very much. I ended up getting a place with some other girls I knew. I was living just outside Rochester, in a town called Chili.

As I am very aware today, "we live, we learn." Being verbally and physically abused every day as a child, with no refuge, is a smothering lifestyle. Then there I was, a teenager trying to protect the other children. What could I do? Where was the escape for a maturing young lady surrounded and living in total darkness? I thought leaving that situation was the answer to my problems, but there were many more challenges to come as I grew older as I will continue to tell you in the next chapter.

Chapter 3

GROWING PAINS

A lot of people everywhere go through horrendous situations, I knew that and still know it. Yet it was no consolation to me (and isn't for anyone) when I was going through those times. I need to share the depth of the pain and abuse, describing how far I had fallen so I can later demonstrate how far God has restored and healed me.

My mother made us feel very guilty about the abuse. It was an ongoing problem until I was 18 years old and finally moved out. My stepdad continually tried to get into my room, but the older I became, the more I fought. I began to invite other problems into my life as I entered a stage of sexual promiscuity, drug use, and two pregnancy terminations. These things tormented me regularly until I became free of all the baggage through Christ. I carried them around like a sack of barbells strapped to my back.

As we continue our journey together in this book, you will see that I have been through challenges throughout my life. I have experienced failed businesses and economic downturns, but here I am, poised and telling my story in hopes that it will help other people. I am currently married to a wonderful man. My husband and I are still not financially established, but it doesn't matter because I know God's going to provide for us no matter what. He always has. But let me go back and continue my story where I left off.

After leaving my dad, I had a whole new set of friends. I was working, but then again, I always worked. I never had a hard time finding a job. Dad got me a job at Eastman Kodak. My responsibilities situated me in the dark room where it was pitch black. You couldn't see your hand in front of your face. I hated it.

I had to get up early to get there, and I kept falling asleep because it was so dark. Eventually, I quit that job and I started bartending, along with other restaurant duties. This is the point in which I met a guy that for the first time I had sex with. I didn't know the guy. It was my girlfriend's boyfriend's friend, and we were at somebody's house. Nobody was home and he talked me into it. Nobody ever paid any attention or acted like they liked me, so I thought, *Why not?* It didn't go well. I hated it.

I had sex for the first time, and I got pregnant. He said he would be there for me, but he wasn't. He totally disappeared. I had no choice but to terminate that pregnancy. My dad and stepmom knew about it because it was Thanksgiving time. I was throwing up and I could not eat anything. I was very sick, and they were not stupid. They guessed what was wrong. It was horrible, I felt terrible. Terminating that pregnancy was a bad choice, but I didn't think I had any other options.

I am against abortion, but I was young, stupid, and promiscuous—and morally clueless. I was convinced that having children at that point in my life was not a good idea. I had one abortion in New York and another one later when I lived in Florida. After I went through that, I started meeting more guys and having more sexual encounters. For lack of a better phrase, I went wild. There was a lot of drinking and partying, and I was having a ball. I felt like I had so much freedom, but it wasn't freedom. I was still a slave to my past. I didn't know what to do with myself because I never had that much freedom before.

I thought this was what living was all about. I was 'adulting,' and had no shame. I was in bliss. The alcohol was dulling the hurts of my childhood. Being around crowds and sleeping with multiple partners boosted my self-esteem. No one could tell me I wasn't living my best life. I had gotten a taste of the real world, and I was not ready to let it go. Things went from bad to worse, but I hadn't got tired of living life my way.

Chapter 4

THE REAL WORLD

I went on a blind date with another friend of my friend (Ed). We started dating, smoking pot, having sex, then we got married. We were in Rochester at the time. He claimed he couldn't find work anywhere in the area. We tried to get by on little to nothing. I worked at a fast-food place for a short time. We moved into an apartment upstairs from my sister's house because she gave us a break on rent. After a while, we moved into a rented house with my second oldest sister. My husband was growing pot up in the attic and when my brother-in-law found out, he told us we had to leave.

We left, and were outside looking in. My husband stuck to his claim that he couldn't find work. We thought we should go to Florida where the job market was better. My father had purchased a home in Florida next door to my grandmother, who lived in Longwood, Florida. We left New York and moved to Florida where my dad rented us a house. Finally, my husband did get a job with Coca-Cola as a delivery man.

He started off not being very honest. He was telling people that he was replacing tanks of

Coke syrup and taking the empties out, but he was not. He was ripping them off. He was telling them that he would leave several full ones, but he wasn't. Most of them were empty. On one occasion when he was messing with a tank, it blew up and hit him in the nose. It cut his nose open, and he was upset because it ruined his face. He quit that job immediately. I had to work two jobs to make ends meet, working at a bowling alley and at a restaurant.

After Ed left Coca-Cola, he was back on the market. He claimed again that he was looking for a job but couldn't find anything. One day my grandmother inquired if he had found a job. I told her, "No, not yet." She said, "I see him walking past the house every day with his fishing pole." He was going down to the pond every day and telling me he was looking for work. He wasn't working; he was out fishing.

There was a day that the police came to our house, and they were looking for Ed. I said, "What's up? He's not here." They told me some people were saying that a man meeting my husband's description has been at the bus stop trying to pick up young girls. I was so naive at the time; I didn't think he would have been doing anything like that. But then shortly after that, I went to the doctor. I thought I had a yeast infection or something, but Ed had given me gonorrhea. I asked him, "What's going on?" He said, "Oh, I had that when I was in the Army. I must have had a relapse." He thought I was really stupid.

The honeymoon-phase had ended. Looking back in the rearview mirror, I wonder how could I have been so clueless and childlike. It's possible I had missed a few signs that would have showed me reality. Here I was a young woman from the state of New York looking to take a bite out of life, and I was deceived and dishonored by my own spouse. It was time to move on, but I had to develop a strategy.

The Bible records many passages that discuss leaving toxic relationships. In my current state of healing, there is one in particular that I like to share with others.

> Don't be fooled: Bad friends will ruin good habits (1 Corinthians 15:33).

I know that now but I didn't know it then. I was still in control of my life, or so I thought. In reality, other things were controlling me and I didn't know how to be set free. Unfortunately, things got worse before they got better as you will continue to learn in the next chapter.

Chapter 5

MOVING ON

My first and only thought after my infection was, *This is the final straw.* We didn't need to be together anymore. I didn't want to divorce him while living in Florida because the only relative I had there was my grandmother. I didn't want to depend on her for anything. I told Ed we should go back to Rochester because I had a lot of family and friends there and that's what we did. We had to move in with his mom at first because we didn't have a solid plan. She, unfortunately, was a loon. After that, I was able to get a new roommate and moved out to live with some really great girls.

Ed and I were married in 1971, but I left him three years later. After that, I slowly started to rebuild my life. We would go to certain clubs, following particular bands. I was obsessed with one guy in a band. We hooked up a few times, but I was never really his girlfriend. I was just one of his girls. Again, I was making bad decisions and suffering the consequences.

My new roommates and I partied a lot. I continued to do a lot of drinking and drugs. I was not doing cocaine at the time, but I did uppers and downers, pot and hash. There were no needles, no heroin, nothing heavy duty, just recreational drugs. I think I did LSD once. I never wanted to do it again.

I enrolled in nursing school when I lived with them. I was working as a waitress at a big facility that had weddings and all kinds of special events. I got paid pretty well, plus I was getting paid to go to school. I was still doing drugs, but I could function. The state had a federally funded program in which they paid us to go to school. We received minimum wage, the objective being that the graduates would enter the job market and pay taxes after graduation. And that's exactly how it happened. It worked. Unbelievably, I got my nursing degree while working at a party house.

There were a lot of different roommates. I went to work at a restaurant outside of Rochester. All the details are fuzzy, but not necessary for the portion of this story. One of my roommates was Mary, the sister of the guy who I was obsessed with, and she and I were very close.

We worked at this restaurant and the cook at the time was a really scruffy guy. He asked if he could borrow $100 or $200 because he wanted to buy some product (cocaine). He promised to pay me back all the money, plus give me some of the product. I was all in. He did the deal. He came back, paid me my money, and gave me the product. Everything was good. I started snorting and liked it a lot. He wanted to do another deal. I fell for it, and we did it again. This next time, he didn't want to pay me back. I had to chase him around town for my money.

One day I spotted him at a place where I was with my friends, and we were listening to a band. He was just sitting there so I went up and I grabbed him by his beard. I told him I wanted my money now. He stood up with a look in his eyes as if he was going to kill me. The guy that was singing up on the stage (a great big black man) was one of my buddies. He stopped singing and was ready to come over and take this guy out for me. When the dealer saw what was getting ready to happen, he left me alone.

This was a demonstration of my ignorance, or maybe I was fearlessly blitzed at that moment. I don't know today what I thought I was going to do with this man. I grabbed his beard and did not have a plan for a counterattack in the works. I was left with no money and no product. The drugs and wantonness were my pleas to be loved. I needed someone to truly love and devote themselves to me. I needed to know that I mattered to someone. I wanted someone to tell me that they needed me. But the problem was I was looking for love despite not knowing what love is.

Chapter 6

A NEED TO
BE LOVED

As the song lyrics went, I was looking for love in all the wrong places. The lifestyle was a textbook case of a woman who had suffered abuse and had no self-worth. Anybody who would pay me any attention, I would follow anywhere. I never really had anybody who I thought really loved me. They used me, but they didn't love me. And I guess I was convinced I was unlovable.

For me, religion was no longer in the picture. There was no church, no praying, no confessions, no communion, no Christian friends, and no religious practice of anything. It was all party, party, and more party. It is my opinion that a lot of the people who struggle with drugs do so because they have no self-worth. I think, if you care about yourself, you're not going to do drugs.

I was looking for something that I thought was going to give me happiness. As a former pastor was fond of saying, "Drugs do give you something, but what they take is more than what they give." Eventually, the drugs stopped giving anything and they just took, took, took, and then took some more.

I graduated from nursing school on July 8, 1977 as an LPN (As I call it, Low Paid Nurse). I went to work at a nursing home for a few years and ran a floor in the home. All the residents loved us. We did a great job. For a period of time, I enjoyed the job. Meanwhile, I met another guy. He was the one who introduced me to heavy-duty coke snorting. I didn't know he had just been released from federal prison for coming back into the country with bags of cocaine strapped to his body. We got heavily into cocaine. Once again, I found myself in an abusive relationship. He broke my nose. I broke his ribs. We fought all the time. With him it was all about getting high, snorting coke, drinking a magnum of Grand Marnier and having sex. But one day I got to the point where I decided I didn't want to do that anymore. Sex was never anything that I sought after or enjoyed. I did it to please my partner.

This is the price I had to pay. This is what I did to myself. But a lot of times it reminded me of my childhood abuse. I tried to escape him, but he would always come after me. Once I had to climb out the bedroom window to get away from him. Another time, he chased me into the bedroom. I got his pistol, and I had it on my chin. I said, "Just leave me alone. Leave me alone." I didn't want him to touch me anymore. He backed up and then I pointed the pistol at *him*! He came and wrestled it from me, and it went off. It didn't hit anyone. It went into the wall of the house.

I finally realized that this was a very unhealthy relationship. In addition to all this activity, I found his glass pipe in a kitchen cabinet, which was evidence that he had been smoking crack cocaine. I had told him many times that if he ever got into that, I was gone. That's when I left.

After this relationship, I got my own apartment above a little house with a nice older couple who lived downstairs. They were super sweet. I went out one night hoping to meet up with this obsession of mine from the band. He was a keyboard player, but he didn't show up. He would always tell me, "We'll meet here, we'll meet there," and I would stand alone without him. On this occasion, I ended up drinking a lot, getting drunk, and going home.

While working at the nursing home, I would collect pills in a big bottle of all the medications that my patients didn't want. I combined Valium, Thorazine, and other medications mixed together. I was done with living, so I took the entire bottle. My good friend, Mary, just happened to come over to my apartment that night with her boyfriend. She found the empty bottle. She tried to wake me up but had to call 9-1-1. They got me out of there quickly on a stretcher, in front of the whole neighborhood! *Good thing I was not aware at the time.*

They took me to the hospital and had to pump my stomach. They put a lot of charcoal in my system to filter some of the toxicity. When I woke up, I was so ticked-off. I screwed this up too.

I couldn't even commit suicide properly. I was so mad. They wouldn't let me leave the hospital until I went through the group therapy, and I promised them I wouldn't try it again. I must've been very convincing because they let me go, but I had every intention of doing it again.

I was striving for an ending, not a new beginning. Building and maintaining a healthy life was not on my agenda when I left the hospital and group therapy. My life had no meaning and, most importantly, I had no respect for myself. Self-care was not in my window of possibility, yet I felt a yearning for determination in the pit of my belly. Little did I know that a change was coming, one that undoubtedly and literally saved my life.

Chapter 7

A NEW BEGINNING

It was then that my sister Rita brought me a book in the hospital written by Dr. Wayne Dwyer titled *Your Erroneous Zones*. I was never an avid reader, but I'm a big fan of the practice today. Simply put, I hate to read. I like to read the Bible, but that's about it. However, I read that book, and it helped me realize that I'm not the only one who messes up. Everyone does. I can't or shouldn't blame myself. It wasn't even a Christian book, but it really hit home with me. I can't be so hard on myself, and the book helped me a lot.

I got out of the hospital, and I had to move in with my older sister, Kathy, who years later passed away. I moved in with her and it was funny because her husband would ask her, "Do we need to hide the aspirin? Do you think she's going to take them all?" I lived with her for a few months. She had two sons and her husband, but they had a nice big house. My biological dad knew everything that had happened that caused my hospital stay. Then one day he said that they were going to take a trip to Florida and asked if I wanted to go with them. I had no car, no job, no life, no apartment—nothing. I had nothing to lose so off we went.

In May 1982 I met up with one of my old roommates from New York who had moved down there with her husband but had since gotten divorced. She said, "Move to Florida and start fresh. You can live with me." I drove back to New York with my dad and packed up one box of what I wanted to take. I had $350 to my name. I flew down to Florida. She not only let me stay with her, she let me use her car to look for a job. I found one and I remember there was a young girl there who tried to witness to me about the Lord, but I just pushed her away. Now I look back and I wish I had listened to her then.

My roommate had a boyfriend, and I was introduced to the boyfriend's friend. We started double dating. He was a nice guy and treated me well. He helped me get some furniture. My roommate and I moved to a different location that was two-bedroom instead of the one-bedroom we had been sharing.

Eventually, my friend moved back to Rochester, and I found another roommate. We became good friends. One night she was out at Bennigan's and was talking to a friend of hers at the bar. She mentioned my name and that I was a nurse. There was a guy sitting next to them. I had already told my roommate about the cocaine dealer up in New York who had abused me. Lo and behold, that guy was at the same bar and somehow he realized they were talking about me. Turns out he had driven all the way down to Florida from Rochester looking for me. He interrupted and said, "Excuse me. Did you say that your friend's name is Jeanette?" She caught on right away. She knew there was something weird.

She said, "No, her name is Janet." He asked, "Is she a nurse?" She made some other profession up and dismissed him. He apparently followed her to our home. The next morning, he was at the front door. I opened the door and said, "What are you doing here?" I tried to shut the door, but he stuck his foot in it to keep it open. I opened it back up and he punched me in the face, right in the nose. I went after him with feet and fists flying. I was able to fend him off and shut the door. When I called the police, their response was that they couldn't do anything because they hadn't seen what happened.

There was another time that I drove to my grandmother's house (pretty far away from where I lived). My car ran out of gas on my way to work, so I got a ride with a friend. When I went back to get my car later that day, the dealer guy had stuck a note on my windshield saying he wanted to talk. I don't know how on earth he found me on that back road. He was obviously stalking me, but I never saw him again after that.

I didn't stay at that first job for long. My nursing license transferred to Florida from New York, so I went to work at a doctor's office in

Winter Park, Florida. It was a general practitioner's office. I worked there for about a year-and-a-half. I then transferred to my OB-GYN doctor's office where there was a team of three different doctors. We rotated working with a different doctor on a weekly basis. I worked there for a couple of years.

I wasn't making a lot of money working in the doctor's office. The nursing job involved taking urine samples, taking blood pressure, getting them in an examination room and giving them a gown. That was not nursing to me. I was disillusioned with that. I eventually looked for another profession and went to work for a builder. They taught me how to work with various programs and other responsibilities. I put all the documentation together for homeowners when they purchased a home. I read blueprints. I learned a lot there, and I liked it.

I was happy with my new position, but there were still missing places in my soul that needed to be filled. I don't think the partying scene was as important to me during this period of my life. I had still been drinking heavily, but I was cutting way back on my recreational drug abuse. Sexual debauchery also became something of the past. It was then that I became focused on something substantial and solid.

Now it is 1984. My new job was with a fairly large home builder. There was a man who would install garage doors for us. He would bring me the keys, and I would put them with the homeowner package. We were all a friendly group. The garage door installer said his son was recently discharged from the Air Force. He also noted that the son was in the process of getting a divorce. He insisted I meet him. I stated, "No thanks." He was not even divorced yet. In my mind, that was the end of that.

One day he came back with his son, Dan. Oh, my gosh! He was so handsome. I thought there was no way that he would be interested in me. I was seven years older than he was, and all the other girls in the office were married so there was not any competition. I was officially introduced to him, and it was a pleasant experience. I said hello and thought that was the end of that.

One of the women who I was working for was having a bonfire at her home and invited me. The next time Dan's father came in, I half-jokingly said to him that I was going to a bonfire and needed a date. He said, "Give me your number and I'll have Danny call you." He talked me into it, so I gave him my phone number. Dan called me that night. We set a date for Saturday night. I suggested that we go out on Friday night first to get to know one another. Of course, I was a little anxious. Friday night came and we went out to a Chinese restaurant and shared one of those big drinks in a bowl. We got along extremely well. We've been together ever since.

When I moved to Florida, I had a steady boyfriend plus a few more before I met Dan. None of them were my idea of someone I wanted to spend my life with. I wasn't doing hard drugs, but I was still smoking pot. I was very happy in

Florida. In New York I was always depressed. The weather was gray, with cloudy skies and wintery weather. I hated that. It was a very depressing area for me. When I came to Florida, my whole life changed. I was very happy.

It was all coming together. The holes were being filled. I started to feel repair, instead of hardcore pain. There had been many men, many sexual relationships in my past. I contribute the looseness to my upbringing. However, life was handing me refuge, strength and courage.

Meanwhile, my friend Dara invited us to church, and it was in an office building in Orlando, Florida. I was raised Catholic, so to me church meant pews, stained glass windows, a crucifix, statues. and the stations of the cross. I looked at it and thought it wasn't a church. We liked it and got more involved with it. We heard the Word, and it resonated with Dan and me, and we thoroughly enjoyed it. We met a couple named David and Ginger Hornsby, and we became good friends. We remain very close friends to this day.

It was a very small church. There were some people there who weren't the most desirable characters, but we understood that church is for everyone. It didn't affect us, but it was different. Again, I was raised Catholic, but Dan identified as a Baptist. It didn't feel like church, but we were getting fed in a way that we had never been fed before. We were getting a good word from the Bible, good Scripture and good teaching. Dan was a lot more familiar with the Bible than me. He dragged me along kicking and screaming.

In 1987, we started going to church under the leadership of Jim Newsom, then John Stanko, and finally Pastor Fred Coller. The church meeting was held on Lee Road in an office complex and then moved from that location to a school in Eatonville, the oldest African American community in the United States. We attended there for quite a while. I remember the church participating in the local Martin Luther King Jr. parade. All the black residents couldn't figure out what all these white people were doing there. It was great fun. I can't say that I knew the Lord then, but I was interested in everything that we were being taught. I was learning to clean up my life.

When Pastor Stanko left, Pastor Fred, an African American, assumed leadership and the church was attended by mostly Black folk. That was fine with us. We loved everyone because we were all like family. But then as things happened, the church changed, times changed, we changed, and after many years we left to attend someplace closer to our home.

I read in *The Upper Room Daily Devotional Guide* that "Even amid life's sudden changes, Jesus offers peace." Our journey had already taken so many twists and turns. We had taken personal hits and now we stood together to battle spiritual attacks. My story continues with a new life in Christ

Chapter 8

MY LIFE WITH DAN

Dan and I went out drinking, not crazy drinking, but more than social drinking. My roommate thought we drank too much. She told us she was worried about us because we were drinking so much. That was a wake-up call for both of us. We cut back. I met Dan in 1985. We got married in 1987, and had our son, Matt, in 1989. We had a small wedding, nothing fancy. We were married in Windermere, Florida. We slowed down on all the drinking. He never wanted me to smoke pot, so I quit doing that.

At the onset, we lived in a lot of homes. My sister teased me that she put my address in her address book in pencil because it is always changing. Dan started working as a stucco laborer, but decided he wanted to have his own business, so we started our own stucco contracting business together. We started with nothing, and it grew into a huge operation with a lot of employees and a large office/warehouse. It grew bigger and bigger every day. Due to the success of the stucco business, we were able to open and operate a Limousine service, a moving company and an Italian Restaurant.

The restaurant was something I had always wanted to do. Dan wanted me to fulfill my dream. Things went smoothly for a bit. My brother was our cook. He, his wife and boys were in it with us. However, he eventually left and went back to selling cars in Fort Myers. It is unfortunate that the restaurant didn't work out. It was a big drain on the business because people were stealing from us. Things got so bad that I had a nervous breakdown and Dan decided we were done. We sold that and took a huge loss on it.

We eventually moved into foam manufacturing; the kind of Styrofoam used for decorative purposes. That also became a huge business. We did work for all the big builders in Florida. We were getting work to be used for condos at the beach. We got a lot of large equipment and put a lot of money into it. We were able to sell the Styrofoam business to someone that happened to inquire about it, and it was an offer we couldn't refuse. We took the proceeds from that sale and reinvested it into our stucco business. Things were looking bright, and we bought a beautiful custom home in an upscale Country Club subdivision on the golf course. We made many improvements to the home, built a nice pool and thought we would live there forever! We lived there for a few wonderful years ... then the economy tanked.

At that point, we lost everything—my car, two boats, and our beautiful house. We had built a house in Arkansas so we could go visit our kids and grandkids. We had a condominium in Palm Coast. We lost it all. All that was so hard to accept and maneuver.

At first, I blamed everything on Dan. I thought he made some bad decisions. I was super close to calling it quits with him but that was my pride making the decision. That was my selfishness because I had finally arrived at a place where I didn't have to work. I could go play golf. I could have lunch with the girls. I could do anything I wanted to do. Now, everything was gone. I didn't know where we were going to live. We only had a certain amount of money to move. Our credit was in the dumper. We had to file bankruptcy. I finally acknowledged that I had enjoyed the good times, therefore, I had to be present for the bad times too. That was a movement of God. I certainly didn't have that attitude in me.

This happened during the real estate collapse of 2008. Home builders had stopped building. They couldn't get loans from the banks. Commercial real estate folded because they couldn't get loans to keep building. We had a lot of leased equipment that we couldn't pay for because we weren't using them. Matt was in school at Florida Atlantic University in Boca Raton, Florida. He lost his scholarship in 2005, at which point we told him he was coming home.

We told him at the start of college that if he messed around and lost his scholarship, we would not be able to bail him out due to our financial situation. He didn't think we were serious, and he was angry with us because we made him get a job. However, to this day, he thanks us for it. Without that discipline, he says that he would not be where he is today.(He is currently operating his own successful insurance business. He has done very well for himself, and we are extremely proud of him. God is so good!)

We were in a desert, thirsty and in need of relief. So much had collapsed around us, we didn't have a current plan to rebuild our lives. We had to readjust our focus. The goal was not regaining our possessions. The lightbulb came on—this was spiritual warfare! And at one point, we found the verse that says,

> "Return to your fortress, you prisoners of hope; even now I announce that I will restore twice as much to you" (Zechariah 9:12).

CHAPTER 9

REBUILDING OUR LIVES

Not only did we lose all our equipment, but we also had to lay off our employees. We had no choice. It was a horrible situation. We felt terrible having to do that. A few of our subcontractors ended up not getting paid. That was another difficult experience. The good news is that I didn't start drinking or doing drugs again. However, I became depressed or maybe just extremely sad. We weren't in a church then, but that's when I needed church the most.

We had a neighbor two doors down from us. We were very good friends when we lived in Redtail. She lost her 29-year-old son around the same time we were going through our storm. I thought I had it bad, but her son had just passed away. That helped put everything into perspective for me. It caused me to realize that I was holding on to the wrong things. I had pangs of guilt for feeling as I did while she was being so strong in the midst of her pain and grief. She and her husband got through it because of their strong faith.

We moved out of our neighborhood. A lot of people didn't make their mortgage payments, but they stayed in their homes. We thought that was wrong, so we moved to New Smyrna Beach, Florida and rented a small condo. I told Dan if we're going to lose everything I want to be at the beach and enjoy what we could. We were across the street from the beach. It was a small place but nice.

During this period, I was not working. Initially, I went to work for a real estate broker, but I didn't have much luck selling anything. Dan took a job with a company selling insulation. It was a commission-based job. They were sending him all over the state. It was hard on both of us. A lot of long hours equaled a lot of stress. Also, he didn't care for the owner of the company.

A friend of ours owned a construction business. His son had gone to school with our son. He hired Dan for part-time work in the remodel division. They were starting a remodeling company and hired Dan to spearhead it. It started part-time, but within two weeks he was full-time and running the show. It was a great job for about seven years.

Then he began looking for something different because he had outgrown his position. Dan put his resume out there and he got a good offer from a company called Ascendant. He did remodeling work because he had obtained a contractor's license. Thank God he was at this job, because that was the only time that we had health insurance.

As it turned out we really needed it at that time. When he had this job, he was diagnosed with prostate cancer in 2019. He had to have surgery that we never could have paid for out-of-pocket.

Dan is good to go as I write, and that insurance made a huge difference. Shortly after that, we started our own remodeling business. We were living in Lake County at the time. During Dan's medical ordeal, I was scared. The test results all came back clear. He did not have any bad symptoms. It was discovered through a blood test, then a biopsy. The surgery was pretty quick, following a lot of testing. We then moved in 2021 to the Tampa area to be closer to Matt and our grandsons.

CHAPTER 10

MY JOURNEY

I have to be honest, I never read the Bible in my life prior to my adult years. I wasn't raised to read the Bible. We just went to religious instructions and went to church on Sunday. Before we left the church I talked about in the previous chapter, the pastor's wife asked me if I would like to go to the ladies' jail with her to speak to the female inmates. I don't know why I said, "Yes," but I did."

We went to the 33rd Street Hotel as we jokingly called it (the jail on 33rd Street in Orlando, Florida). I was a bit intimidated. I arrived and saw ladies sitting there with orange jumpsuits and chains on their legs. I wondered what I had gotten myself into. The pastor's wife asked me to speak so I picked out some good Scriptures to talk about with the women. I had my Scripture references I was going to speak about written out and I thought it sounded pretty good. I began talking.

I forgot about reading what I had prepared because I felt like there was a different reason for me for being there. I ended up giving an abbreviated version of my testimony. Some of the women sat and sobbed. I knew I had a bad situation in my past, but I didn't know it was that bad. But I never knew anything more—I didn't know anything different. After I saw how it affected the ladies, it became clear to me that I went through what I did so I could minister to and help other women. Then, it occurred to me to write a book, but because I was still so ashamed of my past I couldn't imagine telling my story to anyone else—until now more than 35 years later.

The prison visit stirred me, among other things. It wasn't really the thought of a book; it was the vision that I needed to share my testimony with people. I still had many things to learn. The women in the church were helping me to learn to be submissive to my husband. Being a submissive wife was never easy for me. I fought it. Dan had to teach me about tithing because I was a tightwad. My thoughts were, *Heck no, I'm not putting that much money in the basket!* Dan and I would sit in church, and I would quietly argue with him. I couldn't see what he was doing. I questioned his actions. But now, together we tithe with no problems. It was just something I had to learn. (Just like submission!)

Another example of growth is that I love to play cards, especially poker, not so much for the money as it is for the comradery and competition. I was playing cards with a group where I played golf. Some of these people, one person in particular, was not very nice to me. She and I clashed. Another problem I had was the foul mouths of some of the other players. As much as I loved it, I removed myself from the equation. It did not fit into my new life.

I was learning and growing, but I had a long way to go to fill the empty vessels of my heart. My soul still lacked solid structure and a strong spiritual foundation. I was a long way from what Paul wrote in his epistle:

> "When anyone is in Christ, it is a whole new world. The old things are gone; suddenly, everything is new" (2 Corinthians 5:17).

CHAPTER 11

ACCEPTING JESUS CHRIST

I often reflect on my Catholic upbringing because of the lopsided emphasis in my Christian faith now as opposed to when I was young. I was christened as a baby as all Catholic children are. We were never taught about being born again or the need to be baptized as an adult. I always thought there was nothing more for me to do. In 1991, I was water baptized at the home of our pastor, John Stanko, in Altamonte Springs, Florida. I still didn't have a firm grasp on the meaning, but I continued to learn.

After we left the church where I had learned so much, we fell away from church altogether. One day, we decided to go to Northland Community Church and liked it very much. They had great worship services, and we were being fed the Word. We loved it. Then we moved to Lake County from the Orlando area. There was a point when we were involved with a church in our area called Journey. I was baptized again there, and I really felt at that point like I had been born again. That was in 2020, shortly before the pandemic began.

My next-door neighbor Marty and I were good friends. We talked to each other about everything. She played a huge part in my coming back to church and spending time with the Lord. In fact, we had great neighbors who were all Christians. That really helped me to realize that I needed more. I needed to be closer to God. There were so many hurts from my past, and for many years I pushed God away. When I was talking with my neighbor, we'd sit on her front porch swing, and we'd talk, cry, laugh, and share. She really helped my spirit heal and brought me closer to God. When I got baptized the second time, I could really feel the difference. That was huge for me.

Then in 2021 we relocated to the Tampa area to be closer to our son and grandsons. We joined Grace Family Church because our daughter-in-law's family goes to one of their eight locations. During the COVID pandemic, we would watch services online and we loved it. The worship was great. They had different pastors who would speak at different times. It was a wonderful encounter.

We ended up going to the church facility one day because it was not far from our new home, a 15-to-20-minute drive. As soon as we walked into the place, we fell in love with it and started volunteering right away. They have all kinds of groups. I enrolled in a morning *Freedom* class. We are greeters at the door and leaders of the *Connections Team*. (volunteers for the service and offering) I have made so many friends. On Monday nights, there is a group called *Beautiful* that is just for women. Dan attends a group named Courageous, just for men. Everything is awe-inspiring.

We all sit at separate round tables with the same people every Monday night. We share openly and whatever is discussed stays in the group. We pray for each other, and we talk intimately as friends. Sometimes we watch teaching videos. Every gathering is extraordinary, and I love it. I have found a whole new life there. I finally realized that I've had a loving Father all the time.

I also realize that He has forgiven me for all the negative, sinful things of my previous self. The shame is gone. I never wanted to tell my story before because of the shame I felt. Now, that shame is gone. I have forgiven everybody: my stepfather, my mother and other people, including the abusive ex-boyfriend. It had never been in my heart before to even think about forgiving them. This gave me the inspiration for and push to write this book.

Some people would think what I am describing is too good to be true. I didn't believe it either, but it is accessible. Part of it is that you have to have community and fellowship with the right people. I was always in the wrong groups. You have to really dig into the Word. You have to find a decent fellowship in which you're truly being fed. You have to have a good spouse and a good pastor, and we have a group of magnificent pastors. You have to believe that the blood of Jesus has washed you clean, no matter what you have done.

It was always hard for me to believe that. My teacher Debbie in the *Freedom* class drills one fact into my head, "If I can't forgive myself, then I'm not trusting God to forgive me either." If He can forgive me, why shouldn't I be able to forgive myself? Writing and reviewing Scriptures helps a lot. A big change in my life is understanding what God has done for me, and that He has been there all along, but I never knew it. It seems a simple idea, but it's not simple at all. Looking back now, I had to trust in God. I had to believe that He loved me and forgave me. He was and is always there for me. It's like they say, "He never promised you there wouldn't be storms, but He said he would take you through them."

So many things transpired in which I can now positively identify that it was God. Deciding to move to the Tampa area was one of them. We weren't sure that we wanted to move. But now I know we were sent to this house of worship because we needed to be a part of this fellowship with the right people. We had a year-and-a-half lease at our house. We love the house. It was brand new when we moved in. I don't think we'll ever purchase again considering how things are. Our lease was coming up as I wrote, and we were feeling stressed about where we were going to go. We didn't want to get too far from the church. I was in touch with the property management company, and I persuaded them that it would be in their best interest to convince the homeowner to let us stay at the same rent or less. Leases are beginning to creep down a little. When the renewal time came around, we got a small reduction in the rent. And we received a two-year lease extension.

Real estate is not very stable right now as we go to press. I have one listing (I am an agent) and it's for a friend of mine. She's asking for $1.5 million for the property. It will probably never sell. Real estate changes all the time. For employment, I have also been helping Dan. I do a lot of computer tasks, setting appointments, taking phone calls, invoicing, banking, and paying the bills.

I had never been on a mission trip before, so when our church announced it was sending volunteers to Guatemala for a week-long trip, I felt like I was led to join them. I needed to raise the funds to pay for it and I did not know how to do that, but there were people that helped me figure it out. I was able to ask for donations from friends and family, and my financial goal was easily met. It amazed me how generous people can be, and I was thankful for every penny donated, no matter how small the donation was. It warmed my heart that so many people cared enough about my mission to donate.

We were a group of seven women who went. We met once or twice ahead of time to go over the plans, rules, and expectations. I did not get to know any of them very well before we left, but we ended up being close friends and sisters in Christ on the trip.

We got to Guatemala and had a long ride from the airport to the first hotel, and then more long rides to the village we were there to visit. The roads we traveled during the trip went through a lot of rough, mountainous terrain, but our wonderful drivers were experienced at navigating them.

While we were there, we were able to visit people in their homes. We quickly found that they needed so much, and it broke our hearts. We spent time praying with them and loving on them. We even held a "Spa Day." (Actually it was extended to two days. They brought more ladies back the following day because they liked it so much.) We gave the women facials, back/shoulder massages, and painted their nails.

We traveled to other places and learned about their everyday lives, their families, and their daily tasks. We learned all about their coffee business, which amazed us that such demanding work produced such a small profit.

It surprised us how happy the people there seemed, despite their living conditions and lack of basic needs. It made us all realize just how good we have it here in the States. Once I returned home, I was grateful for clean, running water, plenty of food, a warm, comfortable bed, and a lovely home. I pray that I will never take any of that for granted again.

I recently decided to sponsor one of the children I met while there with a monthly donation. It will help with her schooling, and since she is a special needs child, she really requires more attention than the other children we met. The children there only attend school up to the sixth grade, and after that they need to raise enough funds to attend secondary school.

Dan has already been to Cuba on a construction mission trip. We hope to both stay involved with missions as long as we are able. My husband has been such a tremendous asset to my life. I thank God for our meeting and our desire to move forward together. God was the author of our story. He was instrumental in every detail of our relationship. I shudder to think where I would be in my walk without Dan's love and support. In fact, I've asked Dan to contribute a chapter which you will read next.

CHAPTER 12

A WORD
FROM DAN

I am going to try to weigh-in without taking anything away from Jeanette's story.

Jeanette and I started to attend New Hope, a small startup church and we fell in love with the people. The church grew and I was blessed to have Pastor John Stanko as my Pastor. John's teaching was exactly what I needed at the time. We had several good years in church, in marriage and in business. Frankly, these were some of the best times of my life. God protected me and kept good people around me. I had a little bit of community every day because a group of male friends from the church worked with me. However, Jeanette never had that. When we moved to the Country Club and left New Hope, Jeanette's friends were completely different. They were not church people. I had community going for me, but I think the lack thereof hurt Jeanette. We didn't grow apart, however. It's just that I was getting something she wasn't.

I never thought our business ventures would

get to what they became. There was a time in our lives when we were doing $1 million in revenue every month. Then, suddenly, things changed. Our cash flow dropped in half and we realized something was going on. Our dear friend David, our CFO came to me at that point and said, "Are you at least a bit concerned about this?" I optimistically said, "It's just a dip and then we'll be back up and running. We'll be ahead of everybody." I didn't think it was going to last. We were flush with cash. We had three homes. We ended up borrowing against everything we owned. We threw it all at the businesses to keep things running as long as possible and didn't let any employees go until it was evident the economy and our businesses weren't coming back.

I remember sitting one night with Jeanette sitting on my lap crying. I told her I didn't know if we could pull it out. I said, "I know we can get through this. With God's help, we'll get through somehow." I didn't have much more to say than that. We were not in a church fellowship at that time. We had no church and no community. This is what we were lacking. But we had no place to grow with others in community. We had stepped away and positioned ourselves to fight this war alone. I think we purposely ran away for a little bit and began to rely on ourselves instead of the Lord. However, God was in control the entire time. After leaving New Hope Church, we didn't connect to a church right away as I said. Then we went to Northland for a while as Jeanette already wrote. Later we started to plug in at Journey in Apopka. We knew we needed to find a church home. We moved during the Covid pandemic from the Orlando area to the Gulf Coast. It was not the easiest time to evaluate and visit churches. In a way, we were both in search of community but didn't know it. It is important to be with other good, solid Christian people. Scripture says that bad company corrupts good morals. You're not going to maintain an outpost for God if you're hanging around with ungodly people. We were never comfortable in any place until we got to Grace Family Church. We started to feel at home there right away. We were being spiritually fed and the Holy Spirit was able to work through us.

Supporting my wife is as natural as breathing. When she has cracks in her spiritual armor, I surround her in prayer.

> And also use the shield of faith with which you can stop all the burning arrows that come from the Evil One. Accept God's salvation as your helmet. And take the sword of the Spirit—that sword is the teaching of God. Pray in the Spirit at all times. Pray with all kinds of prayers, and ask for everything you need. To do this you must always be ready. Never give up. Always pray for all of God's people (Ephesians 6: 16-18).

When I met Jeanette, she was carrying a heavy load. I did my best to reach her, but her demons could only be dealt with in the spiritual realm. The unforgiveness was such a heavy load for one soul to bear. It is not easy to let go of the past, but to enjoy lasting peace, it is necessary to do so. I love my wife and I'm proud of the progress she has made in the Lord. And I am grateful to God that He did not let go of us in the hard times—and they were hard. He was faithful and stayed true to us.

Now I'll turn it back over to Jeanette to finish up the book.

CHAPTER 13

UNFORGIVENESS

I have come to understand that unforgiveness, the main focus of this book and the key to my freedom, keeps us at a distance from God. I have chosen on purpose to forgive everyone who has hurt or abused me during my lifetime.

> Be gentle and ready to forgive; never hold grudges. Remember, the Lord forgave you, so you must forgive others (Colossians 3:13, TLB).

It is not for the sake of the person who offended you that you need to forgive, but it is for you so you can be set free.

> "But when you're praying, first forgive anyone you are holding a grudge against, so that your Father in heaven will forgive you your sins too" (Mark 11:25 TLB).

Unforgiveness can keep you from having the peace and comfort that God has for you. It may not be easy at first, but if you pray and trust God, you can feel the stillness in your heart when you truly forgive.

There was a point in time when Pastor John

Stanko took me through a deliverance ritual to rid me of the unforgiveness and its accompanying baggage that I was harboring. I had to confess how bitter I was against my mother because of how mean and violent she was, often beating us. I had been trying to get over all that turmoil for years. I was always ashamed for what I was, who I was, or how I did things.

Then the *Freedom* class offered at Grace Family Church has taught me about the penalties of unforgiveness. Further, the class taught me about surrendering things to God which were keeping me from having a good relationship with Him. That also helped me to know that I needed to stay in community with other Christians. For too long, I got involved with groups of people who were not Christians and that didn't help me.

> Be gentle and ready to forgive; never hold grudges. Remember, the Lord forgave you, so you must forgive others (Colossians 3:13, TLB).

I previously suggested that the word *forgiveness* is in the Bible so much because of the need we have to extend it. We see it everywhere in Scripture because it is commanded. For much of my life, I held grudges. Now, good things flood my memory. I've searched my mind and my heart and believe I have settled all accounts. The enemy keeps us in bondage when we hold grudges against those who have hurt us or affected us negatively. It can cause us to harbor anger, bitterness, resentment, or other harmful emotions.

Unforgiveness keeps us from having the peace and comfort that God has for us. It may have taken me a while, but I truly believe in my heart that I am totally forgiven. I have been set free from bondage. It is my prayer that anyone reading this book who has experienced hurts or abuse from another, and harbors ill-will towards those alive or deceased, will ask God to help you to forgive them. Although it is still your decision, it is not for the person, it is for you to set you free. At first, it may not be easy. However, if you pray and trust God, you can feel peace within your heart. The choice is yours and I urge you to make it.

Forgiveness frees you from bondage, and total forgiveness leads to better relationships, improved physical health, mental clarity, emotional healing, and spiritual peace. Jesus commands you to forgive those who wound you seventy times seven times (see Matthew 18:21-22). Forgiving anyone who offends you is how you show grace to others. It is not a single act, but the way God commands you to live on a daily basis. And forgiveness is an ongoing process, for you can forgive but then bitter feelings arise again. At that point, it is necessary to forgive again, and again, and again. Let's look at forgiveness more closely in the next chapter.

CHAPTER 14

FORGIVENESS

As I have already shared, I was always embarrassed and ashamed. Now, having gone through some things and learning more about God's ways, and having gone through the Freedom class, I understand that I don't have to feel ashamed or embarrassed any longer. That's because God isn't ashamed of me. After all these years, I have been set free.

> "Your heavenly Father will forgive you if you forgive those who sin against you; but if you refuse to forgive them, he will not forgive you" (Matthew 6:14-15, TLB).

I got it, if God can forgive me for all my transgressions, how can I not forgive others? It may have taken me a while to understand it, but I truly believe that I have total forgiveness, and I have been set free. I pray that if you have anyone in your life dead or alive who has hurt you or abused you, that you can ask God to help you to forgive them.

> Instead, be kind to each other, tender-hearted, forgiving one another, just as

God has forgiven you because you belong to Christ (Ephesians 4:32, TLB).

The Freedom course was designed to free those who believe the lie from Satan that they're not good enough to receive God's grace or forgiveness. You can be redeemed from the lies that you will never be worth anything, or you won't amount to anything. I have unfortunately heard those statements all my life, first from others and then from my own self-talk. But now I do not feel like there's any shame or condemnation and no reason to be ashamed of what I went through.

People need to know that they can't be ashamed and shouldn't feel bad about themselves. They are worthy of God's favor because they are children of God. They are worth something. The Freedom class I have referred to is for people who need hope. It gives insight into being forgiven for all of the inappropriate things they did or that were done to them. Primarily, it's about not having your life affected by lies, and it encourages faith in God. If your church or one near you offers this course or one like it, I urge you to enroll.

Scripture may be repetitive and is so because we often need the reminder. You can't do this life on your own. You don't wake up one morning and say, "Now I'm going to be a good girl or boy." Condemnation will always creep back in when you fail. Somebody will say something to you to offend or anger you, or a memory will come back to disturb. God says when He forgives, He will remember your sins no more.

Some religious people want to work for their absolution. The Scripture records how people once sacrificed animals to God for the remission of their sins. God is merciful and did forgive their sins, but now there is a better way. He provides grace to us that we do not deserve. The woman caught in the act of adultery, for example, did not get what she deserved as we read in John 8. And later John wrote in one of his letters,

> But if we confess our sins to him, he can be depended on to forgive us and cleanse us from every wrong. And it is perfectly proper for God to do this for us because Christ died to wash away our sins (1 John 1:9, TLB).

I have repented of my sinful lifestyle (turned around from the direction in which I was headed). Confession is agreeing with God that you were wrong, and the things that you did were wrong. He knows it, but He wants to hear you admit it to yourself and to Him also.

When I decided to forgive, I stopped playing the victim. I did not blame anyone else for my problems or sins. Although there were a lot of other people involved. I took personal responsibility for my own actions. I confessed my personal culpability in this process. God not only forgave me, but He cleansed me. I'm a new creature in Christ.

> There was a time when I wouldn't admit what a sinner I was. But my dishonesty made me miserable and filled my days

with frustration. All day and night your hand was heavy on me. My strength evaporated like water on a sunny day until I finally admitted all my sins to you and stopped trying to hide them. I said to myself, 'I will confess them to the Lord.' And you forgave me! All my guilt is gone (Psalm 32:3-5, TLB).

Forgiveness is not a feeling. It is an act of obedience between man and God. There is no choice—you have to forgive—if you want to enjoy the fulness of life God promises. You can look forward to the future with confidence. He has great plans for all of us—including you.

"But when you are praying, first forgive anyone you are holding a grudge against, so that your Father in heaven will forgive you your sins too" (Mark 11:25, TLB).

You can't just look at someone and say, "Oh yeah, I forgive you. It's fine. Whatever." You can't ignore what they did or how you feel. You must leave no room for animosity or ill-will toward the person. You must totally forgive them. Even though my stepfather died years ago, I never really forgave him until 2023. I held on to the bitterness and hatred towards him, and for my mom. They are both gone now but I still had to deal with my own heart.

I did, however, reconcile with my mom before she passed away. I told her I forgave her for putting us at risk and turning her head on things she knew were happening under her roof. I don't know if she received or acknowledged my efforts. I don't think she believed she ever did anything wrong. Forgiveness isn't dependent upon the other person's attitude, behavior, or even acceptance. They are not required to be made aware that you are forgiving them.

If the person who hurt you is deceased, you can't go to them. If they are alive, it can sometimes complicate matters. You want to say, "I forgive you for being such a stupid fool" but that doesn't solve anything. In fact, that's really a way of getting back at them, hurting them for how they hurt you. We may have all thought that way a time or two, but forgiveness is just for you. Forgiveness is not a business transaction in which you do this, and I'll do that. Your forgiving others doesn't depend on them knowing or caring that they hurt you. It can't be based on their sorrow for what they did.

God is my Father and will not bless me if I'm not being obedient and doing the right thing. The Bible is clear. We have tried, in very many cases, to determine how God is going to relate to us. If we are merciful to others, He will be merciful to us. If we forgive others; He will forgive us.

> When you talk, don't say anything bad. But say the good things that people need—whatever will help them grow stronger. Then what you say will be a blessing to those who hear you. And don't make the Holy Spirit sad. God gave you his Spirit as proof that you belong to

Him and that He will keep you safe until the day He makes you free. Never be bitter, angry, or mad. Never shout angrily or say things to hurt others. Never do anything evil (Ephesians 4:29-31).

Our lives will end in eternal death unless God claims us as part of His redeemed flock. Jesus bought us with a price, and we belong eternally in His Kingdom.

CHAPTER 15

REDEMPTION

There is a woman named Hosanna Wong who is an author, speaker, and spoken-word artist. I think she's amazing. At a conference I attended, she put up all these words on a screen to illustrate how God sees us. She asked which we identified with. Before my eyes were phrases like "child of God," "restored," "made new," and other positive expressions that I never felt were part of my reflective image.

I used to rationalize and make excuses for everything I was doing. Deep down, I knew it was wrong, but I'd never really admitted it and never confessed it to God. What's more, I felt powerless to get out of it. Even though I would confess to doing wrong, I would go back the next night and do it all over again. I was in a downward spiral of condemnation, guilt, anxiety, and frustration. There was no way out until I called out to the Lord.

Trials and issues may endure. They are part of being alive. Through it all, He remains by our side. Because of the love, the presence, and power of God and our faith in Him, we not only survive, but we also thrive. He never left me. He loved me enough to bring me through it all despite my ongoing wrong responses. At the time, I didn't understand why I was going through all those traumas. Nevertheless, I was not alone; God was always with me. When I was weak and hopeless He held on to me as His child and made me strong.

Sometimes I feel that I can do more in certain situations. Admittedly, I am limited. I must rely on His strength, not my own.

> "For I know the plans I have for you, says the Lord. They are plans for good and not for evil, to give you a future and hope. In those days when you pray, I will listen. You will find me when you seek me, if you look for me in earnest" (Jeremiah 29:11-13, TLB).

As a young girl, I knew there was a God, but I didn't think He knew me. Faith is what got me to this stage of healing and wholeness because I no longer believe the lies that Satan has led me to believe. There were times I didn't feel like I was going to make it. As a child, I prayed every night that something would change. I was desperate for help but there was no help anywhere, except the help I didn't realize I was already receiving. He held on to me when I tried to take myself out, but He didn't allow it.

> "Fear not, for I am with you. Do not be dismayed. I am your God. I will strengthen you; I will help; I will uphold you

with my victorious right hand" (Isaiah 41:10, TLB).

I had many fears. I was afraid of my mother. I was afraid of my stepfather. I was afraid of staying alive. I was afraid of trying to survive. I was afraid of going to hell. I was afraid of almost everything. God gave me strength to survive and now His grace allows me to thrive.

The way we treat others is the way He is going to treat us. While all this is grace and mercy of God, we still have a role to play in this transaction. We still have to make good decisions and as we do, God will renew our will so we can grow and mature to make better decisions. He will strengthen us and make us a new creation, but we must cooperate and obey.

I now know without a doubt that I am a child of God, and He has always been my one, true loving Father. I lean on the word of God who says who I am, not what I have always been told that I am. When you start to believe who God says you are, He will lead you into freedom.

CHAPTER 16

AT THE CROSS

As of August of 2024, Dan and I have been married for 37 years. My husband is very good to me. We have an awesome son who is married to Riana, a wonderful woman. I am a grandmother and a great-grandmother. It is suddenly a new world. My walk is a new adventure that I didn't know was possible. I feel as if I have lived about five or six different lives. All the phases of my existence have been a different life. Dan and I pray together a lot. We come together for direction and decisions. We ask for guidance regarding both business and our Christian Walk. We didn't do this years ago.

I don't know how many chapters I have left in my life. I turned 73 in 2024. My mainstay Bible verse that has helped me through is a popular one:

"I can do all things through Christ who strengthens me (Philippians 4:13, NKJV).

I never thought I could accomplish anything. If I leaned on my own abilities or understanding, I wouldn't have even attempted to do certain things. Now I know that I can do all things because if it's God's will, He's going to help me through it. He's going to help me and give me strength.

I recently started playing golf again. I played with this woman who nobody likes because she is rude, mean, and nasty to others. God's grace and mercy allowed me to fellowship with her. There were moments that I wanted to throat punch her, but I kept my mouth shut. My husband will attest to the miracle of me being able to control my tongue. I had no filter sometimes in the past, but I'm getting better.

I no longer try to control circumstances. I can deal with things that I couldn't deal with before because I gave my heart and will over to God. It's not me. Twenty years ago, I would have been undone. God has done something in my life. Some would acknowledge that this is what a test is called. He's tested me to show the strength of what it is that He can do in a person's life.

Sometimes I will start to give a testimony in my *Freedom* class, and I begin to cry. It's not because I feel bad about what I went through. It is because I can't believe that I've been set free from all of it, and that I am forgiven, I am loved, and I have a father. I cry tears of joy. I trust that God will put this in the hands of other people who say I'm where she was, and I want to be where she is now. I want God to use my story.

> So, there is now no condemnation awaiting those who belong to Christ Jesus. For the power of the life—giving

Spirit—and this power is mine through Christ Jesus—has freed me from the vicious circle of sin and death (Romans 8:1-2, TLB).

I think a lot of why I never shared my story was because I could not forgive myself. Now, there's no condemnation. I'm over it. This is why I'm putting it out there currently. I react differently to things now. God has set me free from the vicious cycle of sin and death. I feel like a number one in God's eyes. I'm not the same person I once was. I don't do the same things I used to do. I associate with different people, and I don't feel bad about myself. I may sometime say something that's not perfectly Christian, but I'm not condemning myself for it. And now I know God doesn't either.

Sin is sin. I would tell others that they have not done anything any worse than anyone else. Those sins are forgotten and forgiven in Jesus' eyes if we ask them to be so. Nothing shocks Him. He knows what we are going to do before we do it. Jesus died for us, to provide a way for us to escape the condemnation and effects and penalty of sin. It took me a long time to realize this. But now, I know the truth. I realize my bondage were all lies from Satan, and I don't have to believe them anymore. God doesn't see those things. It is amazing. We may still talk about these things. They are not totally erased from our memory. They happened, but to Him they do not exist anymore. The slate has been wiped clean. The sin has been erased from the record books. There are still things that I know I was wrong in doing. However, I no longer carry the guilt and shame.

I take this time to interject a relevant story told to me by Pastor Stanko:

> *"A man had a friend, and they were in prison together. They both got out, got married, and had kids. One was a very successful paralegal aide. Unfortunately, he got back into drugs and got busted. When he appeared in court, the judge said, 'Sir, I'm embarrassed, but we have looked for your past records. We cannot find anything. Therefore, as far as this court is concerned, you are now standing before this court with your first offense. I therefore give you probation. Don't do it again.' He knew what it was like to stand justified before the tribunal of God. An easy way to remember justified is 'just as if I've never sinned.'"*

"Don't copy the behavior and customs of this world but be a new and different person with a fresh newness in all you do and think. Then you will learn from your own experience how his ways will really satisfy you" (Romans 12:2, TLB).

I feel brand new. I think new thoughts. I do new things. I associate with new people. I no longer do what I used to do. I have learned that I don't need the old ways to satisfy me. I am very satisfied when I feel like I'm doing the right thing. I like helping people. Most essentially, I have learned to keep my mouth shut.

I have broken my connection with the world. I still go golfing and do some other things, but I no longer take my cues or lessons from the world's system of things. I don't have one foot in the Kingdom of God and the other foot out.

> He has removed our sins as far away from us as the east is from the west (Psalms 103:12, TLB).

I have heard it said many times already, but it bears repeating. The sins that we feel convicted of from our past (or present) are removed. These words are comforting. It's like the woman who was caught in adultery as told in John 8. Jesus told her to go her way and sin no more. He told her that there was no one to condemn her so He did not condemn her either. This is an act of God. This is nothing you can do under your own power. This is a benefit of putting faith in Christ. It's a great transaction. He takes an old set of worn-out tires (your life) and gives you a brand-new set with no holes in them or wear on them. That's a great deal and it's free.

God is willing to accept and redeem you. I convicted myself of my own sin. When I talk of my testimony, I usually break down. I don't feel sorry for myself or for what I have been through. You wouldn't believe how grateful I am for God's mercy, grace, and forgiveness. It's sometimes overwhelming, but nevertheless amazing.

> "And I will be merciful to them in their wrongdoings, and I will remember their

sins no more" (Hebrews 8:12, TLB).

It is just that plain and simple, almost too good to be true. And I am now living a life too good to be true but true and available to me and all those who call on God to help them. If you have done that, you know what I mean. If you haven't, I urge you to do so without waiting another minute to be free from your past so you can fully embrace your future in God.

FINAL THOUGHTS

After all these years, I have finally realized that God has always been my one true Father. He has never left me, even though I turned my back on Him at times. The truth is, I am a child of God and He loves me no matter what. I am no longer listening to the lies I have been believing about myself. I never felt "good enough" but I know now that I am, because I know who He is. He doesn't make mistakes, and I am exactly who He intended me to be. I still have a long way to go, but with faith I know I can get closer to Him and try my best to be more like Him.

www.ingramcontent.com/pod-product-compliance
Lightning Source LLC
Chambersburg PA
CBHW062026040426
42447CB00010B/2164